Pygora Goats Care

Pygora Goats Care

A Complete Owner's Guide to Raising
Pygora Fiber Goats as Pets

Facts about Pygora Goat Breeding, Lifespan, Personality, Fiber
Uses, Health Problems, Diet and Showing Information

Pygora Goats Care

A Complete Owner's Guide to Raising Pygora Fiber Goats as Pets

Facts about Pygora Goat Breeding, Lifespan, Personality, Fiber Uses, Health Problems, Diet and Showing Information

Author: Taylor David
Published by: Windrunner Pets
windrunnerpets.com

ISBN: 978-1-927870-62-4

In this book, you will find all of the information you need to be prepared for becoming a Pygora Goat owner. You will find information about Pygora Goat care, care sheet, cages, enclosure, habitat, diet, facts, set up, food, names, pictures, info, life span, breeding, feeding and cost. After reading this book you will be an expert on Pygora Goats!

Acknowledgements

I would like to thank my family for supporting me as I researched and wrote this book. They are also the ones who help me to care for my own herd of Pygora Goats – I couldn't do it without them!

Table of Contents

Chapter One: Introduction

If you hadn't heard of the Pygora Goat until recently, don't worry – you are not alone. The Pygora Goat is a fairly rare and unique breed that is still gaining popularity in the United States. In fact, the breed only originated in 1987 so it has been in existence for less than 30 years! As you may have guessed from the name, the Pygora Goat is a cross between the Angora and the Pygmy Goat, two popular types of domestic goat often kept as pets.

Pygora Goats are more than just pets, however, they also produce luxurious fiber. This fiber may be similar to cashmere fleece or mohair in texture – it could also be a combination of the two. These beautiful animals come in a variety of colors and they are loved for their fiber as well as their gentle personalities.

In this book, you will learn more than just the basics about this wonderful breed – you will learn everything you need to know to raise and care for Pygora Goats. Within the pages of this book you will find information regarding deciding whether a Pygora Goat is the right choice for you, where to buy one, how to care for your goats and even tips for showing them. After reading this book, you will be an expert on all things related to the Pygora Goat!

Useful Terms to Know

Abomasum – The second largest chamber of a ruminant's stomach – this is where digestion actually occurs

Banding – A castration technique used on farm animals in which an elastic band is placed around the testicles, cutting off blood flow

Bleat – The name for the vocal expression of a goat

Browse – Woody plants, shrubs or brush with broad leaves – common grazing material for goats

Buck – A male goat, also referred to as a Billy

Buckling – A young male goat, intact, under 1 year of age

Butting – A behavior exhibited by male goats, often in play, using the top of the head

Capriculture – The art of goat husbandry

Colostrum – The first milk produced by a doe – a vital source of nutrients and antibodies for the kids

Dam – Female parent of a goat

Doe – A female goat, also referred to as a Nanny

Estrus – The period of time lasting from one heat cycle to the next

Estrus Cycle – A series of cycles during which a female goes into heat, typically July through February

Herd – A group consisting of more than one goat

Kids – The offspring of a goat, baby goats

Manger – A feeding trough

Rumen – The largest chamber of a goat's stomach

Ruminant – An animal with a 3- or 4-chambered stomach

Sire – The male parent of a goat

Wether – A castrated male goat, incapable of breeding

Yearling – A young goat between 6 and 12 months of age

Chapter Two: Understanding Pygora Goats

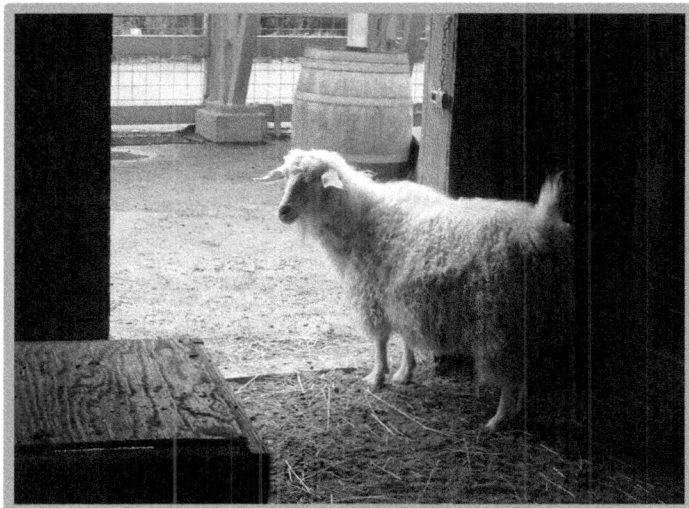

Before you decide whether a Pygora Goat is the right pet for you, you need to learn a little bit about them. In this chapter, you will find all the basic information you need to know about this breed including what they are, some facts about them and their history as pets. You will also find information regarding how they compare and contrast with other types of domestic goats including the Pygmy Goat, the Angora Goat and the Cashmere Goat.

1.) What Are Pygora Goats

The Pygora Goat is the result of an Angora Goat being bred with a Pygmy Goat. These goats are not considered true Pygoras until the second generation – in order to be considered a true Pygora, the goat must have no more than 75% of either Angora or Pygmy history. This breed is a unique blend of characteristics from both types of goat. It grows the long, soft fiber of the Angora but maintains a size closer to that of the Pygmy.

Another notable fact about Pygora Goats is that they are frequently kept as pets in addition to the traditional purposes of showing the goats and using them to produce fiber. Angora goats are known for their placid natures while Pygmy goats have a bit more spunk. The Pygora Goat combines the characteristics of both, having a friendly and easy-to-handle temperament with an attitude of playfulness.

2.) Facts About Pygora Goats

The Pygora Goat is a medium-sized breed of domestic goat. As you have already learned, this breed is the result of a cross between a Pygmy Goat and an Angora Goat. These goats have soft, luxurious fiber that comes in one of three types:

Type A: Mohair-like, shiny ringlets about 6 inches (15 cm.) long; fiber does not shed, it must be plucked or shorn

Type B: A blend of A and C fiber, wavy with curls at the end of the locks; soft and fluffy, 3 to 6 inches (7.6 to 15 cm.) in length; goats with this fiber will blow their coats

Type C: Cashmere-like fiber, crimped and wavy with little curl; matted look, between 1 and 3 inches (2.5 to 7.6 cm.) in length; goats with this fiber blow their coats

In addition to having different types of coats, Pygora Goats also come in a variety of colors – white, black, brown, red and gray or any of these colors diluted with white. Because both Pygmy and Angora Goats are horned, the Pygora Goat is born horned as well. Both horned and de-horned goats are acceptable for show by the Pygora Breeders Association (PBA), however. Many got owners prefer to de-horn their goats to prevent them from injuring themselves or other goats.

Pygora Goats are naturally social animals – like other goats – and are best kept in herds. Though a herd is technically defined as a group consisting of more than one goat, a group of three or more is recommended. You should not, however, plan to keep intact males together with female goats. Castrated males, called wethers, are the ideal companions for an intact buck while females can be kept in groups with others of the same sex.

At birth, Pygora Goats weigh only about 5 lbs. (2.2 kg.) but, within minutes, they are able to stand and nurse. In as little as four hours, Pygora Goat kids are able to jump and play. Pygora Goats reach sexual maturity between 8 and 12 months of age – at this point it is safe to breed them as long as you can accommodate and care for the kids. The breeding season for these goats typically spans the period between July and February and the gestation period is around 145 to 150 days. These goats can give birth to between one and four kids with each breeding, though it is very common for them to have twins.

When they are full grown, female Pygora Goats stand at least 18 inches (46 cm.) tall and weigh between 65 and 75 lbs. (29 to 34 kg.). Males are larger, standing at least 23 inches (59 cm.) tall and weighing between 75 and 95 lbs. (34 to 43 kg.). The average lifespan of this breed is between 12 and 14 years, though some goats have been known to live longer. The Pygora Goat is friendly and playful by nature, but easy to handle. For these reasons, they make excellent pets.

If you do plan to keep Pygora Goats as pets, realize that shearing them will be part of your responsibility. The fiber produced by these goats can be spun into thread or yarn for use in many projects – you can even sell it. Pygora Goats with fiber types B and C will shed their coats in the spring (type A will not), but it is a shame to let that fiber go to waste. Most goat owners choose to shear their goats in the late winter, as long as the temperature is not too low.

Summary of Facts

Scientific Name: *Capra hircus hircus*
Goat Type: Fiber
Fiber Types: mohair, cashmere, blend
Height (Does): at least 18 inches (46 cm.)
Height (Bucks): at least 23 inches (59 cm.)
Weight (Does): 65 to 75 lbs. (29 to 34 kg.)

Weight (Bucks): 75 to 95 lbs. (34 to 43 kg.)

Colors: white, black, red, cream, brown, gray

Temperament: friendly and playful

Handling: gentle and easy to handle

Lifespan: 12 to 14 years average

Sexual Maturity: 8 to 12 months

Gestation Period: 145 to 150 days

Offspring: one to four, often twins (2)

Other Uses: therapy animals, companion animals, pets

3.) History of Pygora Goats as Pets

Goats have been domesticated for thousands of years, but it hasn't been until the last few hundred years that they have gained popularity as pets. Several breeds of domestic goats are popularly kept and bred for their milk, fiber and meat but many are kept exclusively as pets. The Pygora Goat is a fairly new breed, having only been developed within the last half century. This breed is a popular pet, but it can also be kept for its fiber.

The history of the Pygora Goat begins back during the 1980s when Katharine Jorgensen, an NPGA Pygmy Goat breeder and 4-H judge, wanted to create a colored mohair goat. Pygmy Goats have a colored cashmere-like undercoat, but the fiber is too short to use for spinning yarn or thread. In order to create the goat with the qualities she desired, Jorgensen bred an NPGA Pygmy doe to an AAGBA Angora buck. The result was a group of fluffy white kids.

This group of kids had a unique type of fiber – one that wasn't quite mohair or cashmere. After several generations of breeding, Jorgensen came to identify three specific types of fiber. Type A was similar to mohair while Type C was similar to, and could be sold as cashmere. Type B was a combination of the two – wavy rather than curly but still soft and fairly fine.

As enthusiasm for the new breed spread, Jorgensen needed to settle on a name. She originally intended to name the new breed Homestead Goats since they were large enough to produce fleece and milk as well as goat meat. She eventually decided, however, to combine the names of the parent breeds to create the new breed name: Pygora. In 1987, she began the Pygora Breeders Association (PBA) with ten members.

In the early years, the PBA set out to track geneology and to develop the breed to follow consistent traits. Jorgensen started a registry and started putting out a newsletter. By 1990, she was ready to form a committee to write the breed standards and by-laws for the association. Part of these breed standards insisted that true Pygoras be bred from registered NPGA Pygmies and AAGBA Angoras. This being the case, the only accepted colors for Pygoras are white (like the Angora) and the colors seen in Pygmy Goats.

Today, the Pygora Goat has grown in popularity. It is now kept as a pet but also kept for its fiber – and even milk production.

4.) Types of Domestic Goats

a.) Pygmy Goat

The Pygmy Goat is one of the parent breeds for the Pygora Goat and it is a breed of miniature domestic goat. These goats are primarily kept as pets, though they can also produce milk. Pygmy Goats are known to be hardy animals, well able to adapt to a variety of climates. This breed is known to be docile and good-natured, as well as alert and very active at times.

Pygmy Goats generally weigh between 50 and 90 lbs. (24 to 40 kg.) at maturity, growing between 16 and 23 inches (41 to 58 cm.) tall. Coat colors include white, caramel, grey, black and agouti. A Pygmy Goat is born with horns and a beard, though some owners choose to dehorn the goats while they are very young.

b.) Angora Goat

The Angora Goat the second parent breed of the Pygora, is known for producing a white, lustrous fiber called mohair. This fiber tends to average about 6 inches (15 cm.) in length. The Angora Goat is a fairly large breed, rather robust and able to live in a variety of conditions. This breed weighs an average of 180 to 225 lbs. (81 to 102 kg.) for bucks at maturity. Females average about 70 to 110 lbs. (32 to 50 kg.).

The fleece of the Angora Goat tends to grow in tight ringlets, though some develop a flatter mohair. Not only are

Angoras valued as fiber-producers and pets, but they make great foraging animals on large properties. Perhaps the largest downfall of this breed is its extreme susceptibility to internal parasites. They are also fairly delicate at birth and need to be protected from cold and damp during their first few days of life.

c.) Cashmere Goat

A Cashmere Goat is one of many breed which produces cashmere wool. This type of wool is very fine and soft, often used for clothing. The fleece actually consists of two types of fiber – cashmere and guard hair. In many cases, the percentage of actual cashmere is around 20%. These goats can produce as much as 2.5 lbs. (1.1 kg.) per year.

Some of the breeds of goat that produce cashmere include:

Australian Cashmere Goat

Changthangi Cashmere Goat

Hexi Cashmere Goat

Alashanzuoqi White Cashmere Goat

Inner Mongolia Cashmere Goat

Liaoning Cashmere Goat

Luliang Black Goat

Licheng Daqing Goat

Tibetan Plateau Goat

Zhongwei Cashmere Goat

d.) Nigerian Dwarf Goat

The Nigerian Dwarf Goat is a miniature dairy breed originating in West Africa. These goats have short, soft coats in any color or combination of colors. The ideal weight for these goats is about 75 lbs. (34 kg.) and they can be disqualified from the show ring if they exceed this amount. Does reach a maximum height of 22.5 inches (57 cm.) while bucks max out around 23.5 inches (60 cm.).

Because this breed looks very similar to the Pygmy Goat, potential owners often wonder what the difference is. In addition to being two separate breeds, the Pygmy is bred for a cobby overall appearance while Nigerian Dwarf Goats are bred to the structure and proportion of dairy goats. Color is another factor because Nigerian Dwarf Goats come in so many patterns and colors – you can never be sure what the offspring of any given pairing will look like.

Chapter Three: What to Know Before You Buy

After reading a bit about the Pygora Goat, you may think you are ready to buy one. In this chapter, however, you will learn that there are a few more things you need to know. Do you need a license to keep goats? How many should you buy? And do they get along with other pets? You will find the answers to these questions and more in this chapter.

1.) Do You Need a License?

Before you buy a new pet, it would be wise to make sure there are no restrictions on that animal in your area. Certain countries and regions prohibit the keeping, breeding or transporting of certain animals based conservation status, whether they are dangerous, and other factors. Below you will find information about licensing requirements for Pygora Goats in both the U.S. and the U.K.

a.) Licensing in the U.S.

While there are no federal laws restricting the possession or breeding of these goats, some states require individual owners to file an application for a license or permit. In most cases, domestic goats are classified as "domestic animals" rather than "wildlife," so keeping of these animals is not prohibited. You should, however, check with your local council to see whether certain zoning restrictions apply.

Depending where you live, zoning regulations may require you to set aside a certain amount of space for your goats. You may also need to post a sign to let your neighbors know that you intend to purchase and keep goats. One of the most important regulations you may be required to follow is in regard to the method of enclosure. Certain cities like Chicago and Seattle have begun to allow the keeping of certain goats as long as they are properly contained.

If you aren't sure whether goats are allowed in your city or not, contact your local zoning department. Many cities have zoning regulations prohibiting farm animals like cows, horses and sheep but Pygora Goats may be considered small animals, in the same category as cats and dogs.

Ask for a copy of the zoning regulations to see whether goats are specifically mentioned and whether there are any requirements for keeping them – for example, a minimum lot size may be required to keep goats. If you are able to determine that goats are not allowed in your area, do not despair. It may be possible to get a formal exemption --- contact your local council to inquire about the process for obtaining one.

b.) Licensing in the U.K.

The legal requirements for keeping Pygora Goats in the U.K. are much more extensive than they are in the U.S. The reason for this is that the Animal Welfare Act of 2006 introduced legal requirements regarding the responsible care and keeping of animals. In order to uphold the Act, a number of legal requirements were put into place – these requirements apply to all goat owners in the U.K.

The Animal Welfare Act 2006 states that an animal's basic needs include:

- A suitable environment
- A suitable diet
- The ability to exhibit normal patterns of behavior
- Protection from pain, suffering, disease and injury
- Appropriate housing with or apart from other animals

In addition to providing for the basic needs of your Pygora Goats, you must also comply with several legal requirements. Before you purchase your goats, you must obtain a holding number (CPH) and a herd number – application for these numbers is free and can be filed with your local Department for Environment, Food and Rural Affairs (DEFRA) office. In addition to obtaining these numbers, you must also keep medical records of individual goats as well as a holding register.

When purchasing your goats, the breeder or seller is required to obtain an Animal Movement License (AML) – this license must be filled out before moving the animal. The only exception for obtaining this license is for taking the goat to the vet. Once you take up ownership of the goat, it is your responsibility to file an AML every time you move the goat off your property such as to shows or for sale.

Before a goat can be sold, it must be identified with an ear tag. The tag must include the herd number as well as a number for the individual animal. Starting in 2008, goats are required to have two forms of identification – one ear tag and a second form of identification, either another ear tag or an ear tattoo. When you tag the goat, you must record the date in your holding register.

Finally, when one of your goats dies, you must record the date in your holding register. You must then have the goat removed from the premises by a licensed collector or you must take the goat yourself to a pet crematorium. As of 2011, it is now legal for goat owners to keep the ashes of their cremated pets. All of these laws are in place to ensure the safety of domestic animals and to prevent the spread of disease.

2.) How Many Should You Buy?

Like most domestic goats, Pygora Goats are social animals. It is not recommended that you keep a single goat on its own – these animals do best in duos or herds. You should be careful, however, with keeping multiple goats of the same sex (male) together. Below you will find recommendations for keeping intact males, females and wethers.

Intact Males = should not be kept with females or other intact males; best kept with a wether for companionship

Females = should be kept with at least 1 other female or wether for companionship

Wethers = should be kept with at least 1 other wether or female goat for companionship

3.) Can Pygora Goats Be Kept with Other Pets?

Pygora Goats are very friendly and playful by nature. This being the case, they are unlikely to fight with other animals. You should be careful, however, when keeping them with other pets. Dogs, no matter how gentle they seem, may chase goats and can even injure them severely. If you have a dog, be sure to supervise its interactions with your goats very carefully. These goats do tend to get along well with other livestock. This includes other types of domestic goats, sheep and cows. If you live on a farm and are able to provide a great deal of pasture space, do not hesitate to let your goats mingle with the other livestock as long as you do not notice any problems.

4.) Ease and Cost of Care

Before you make your final decision regarding whether Pygora Goats are the right choice for you, take the time to consider the cost of keeping them. In this section, you will find an overview of both the initial and monthly costs for keeping Pygora Goats. Only if you are able to cover all of these costs comfortably should you purchase a Pygora Goat.

a.) Initial Costs

Some of the initial costs to consider when purchasing a Pygora Goat include the enclosure, shelter, the purchase price, necessary veterinary procedures, vaccinations and equipment/accessories.

Enclosure

Depending on the zoning requirements for your region, you will probably need to build an enclosure for your Pygora Goats if you do not already have a livestock enclosure in place. The cost for this varies greatly depending on the size of the pasture you intend to enclose and the materials you use. It is important that you choose quality fencing material to keep your goats in and predators out – you may also want to make sure the fence is high enough that your goats can't jump over it. You should expect to pay between $100 and $1,000 (£65 to £650) to build an enclosure for your goats.

Shelter

The type of shelter you need for your goats will depend on the climate in which you live. Pygora Goats do not like to get wet, so you will need some kind of shelter with a roof. These goats do not do well in four-walled enclosures, but you should provide something like a small barn or a large dog house, particularly if you live in a cold climate. The cost for shelter may range from $50 to $300 (£32.50 to £195) depending on size and materials.

Purchase Price

Pygora Goats range in price depending on age, sex and breeding. For example, a wether may be less expensive than other goats, averaging around $150 (£97.50). Registered bucks, on the other hand, may cost between $150 and $250 (£97.50 to £162.50) while a registered doe might cost from $250 to $300 (£162.50 to £195). If the goat doesn't come with a health certificate, you may need to buy one for around $50 (£38).

Veterinary Procedures

Depending on the age of the goat you purchase, or if you are breeding the goats yourself, you may need to cover the cost of some veterinary procedures. One procedure is disbudding – removing the horns from goat kids before they grow in. To have a vet perform this procedure may cost between $50 and $75 (£32.5 to £49) – you can also purchase a disbudding iron for around $100 (£65) to do the procedure yourself. If you are raising goat kids, you might also need to have them neutered. Again, the cost depends on the method you choose but if you have a vet perform the procedure, it generally costs between $50 and $75 (£32.5 to £49) per goat.

Vaccinations

The cost for goat vaccinations varies depending whether you have a veterinarian administer the vaccines or if you do them yourself. If you buy the vaccine and administer it yourself, it could cost as low as $5 (£3.25)– a veterinary visit to administer the vaccine, however, could cost $30 (£19.50) or more.

Equipment and Accessories

Some of the equipment and accessories you should plan to buy for your goats include hoof trimmers, water and food troughs and shearing equipment if you plan to use your goats for fiber. Costs for equipment and accessories may range from $20 to $250 (£13 to £162.50).

Cost	Wether	Buck	Doe
Enclosure	$100-$1,000 (£65 to £650)	$100-$1,000 (£65 to £650)	$100-$1,000 (£65 to £650)
Shelter	$50- $300 (£32.5 - £195)	$50- $300 (£32.5 - £195)	$50- $300 (£32.5 - £195)
Purchase Price	$100 (£97.50)	$150-$250 (£97.5 - £162.5)	$250-$300 (£162.5 - £195)
Vet. Procedures	$100-$150 (£65-£97.5)	$50-$75 (£32.5 to £49)	$50-75 (£32.5 to £49)
Vaccination	$5-$30 (£3.25-£19.5)	$5-$30 (£3.25-£19.5)	$5-$30 (£3.25-£19.5)
Accessories	$20-$250 (£13 - £162.5)	$20-$250 (£13 - £162.5)	$20-$250 (£13 - £162.5)
Total	$375-$1830 (£26-£1124)	$375-$1905 (£244-£1239)	$375-$1905 (£309-£1271)

b.) Monthly Costs

Some of the monthly costs of keeping and caring for Pygora Goats include food, veterinary care, medications and other additional costs.

Food

Because Pygora Goats are small, they do not need as much food as other types of livestock. The kinds of food you need to provide include hay, grain and alfalfa pellets. A single bale of hay costs between $3 and $10 (£2-£6.5) and one bale, depending on the size, should last a single goat one month. Goat feed, such as grain or alfalfa pellets, costs between $10 and $15 (£6.50-£9.78) per month while the cost of mineral supplements is about $5 (£3.25) per month. Add all of these costs together and you may be looking at an average cost between $18 and $30 (£12-£19.50) per goat per month.

Veterinary Care

As long as you care for your goats properly, you should not have to worry about veterinary care on a regular basis. If you provide a healthy diet, properly administer vaccinations and hoof trimming yourself, you may only need to consult a veterinarian in cases of emergency or illness. Assuming this to be the case, you may want to prepare for an average cost between $50 and $250 (£32.5 - £162.5) which averages to $4 – $21 (£3 - £13.5) per month.

Medications

Pygora Goats do not require many medications. One thing you may want to give them, however, is de-worming medicine which typically costs about $60 (£39) per year which averages to $5 (£3.25) per month.

Additional Costs

Some additional costs you may need to pay on a monthly or yearly basis include the cost of bedding, repairs to the enclosure and replacement of tools and equipment. On a monthly basis, these costs should not be more than $15 to $30 (£9.75 - £19.5).

Cost	Wether	Buck	Doe
Food	$18- $30 (£12-£19.5)	$18- $30 (£12-£19.5)	$18- $30 (£12-£19.5)
Veterinary Care	$4 – $21 (£3 - £13.5)	$4 – $21 (£3 - £13.5)	$4 – $21 (£3 - £13.5)
Medications	$5 (£3.25)	$5 (£3.25)	$5 (£3.25)

Additional Costs	$15-$30 (£9.75 - £19.5)	$15-$30 (£9.75 - £19.5)	$15-$30 (£9.75 - £19.5)
Total	$42 - $84 (£28 - £56)	$42 - $84 (£28 - £56)	$42 - $84 (£28 - £56)

5.) Pros and Cons of Pygora Goats

Before making your final decision regarding Pygora Goats as pets, take the time to familiarize yourself with the pros and cons of this breed. Below you will find a list of both the advantages and disadvantages of Pygora Goats as pets. Use this information to guide you in your decision.

Pros for Pygora Goats

- Smaller size than other livestock, easier to keep on smaller properties
- Friendly and gentle by nature, good pets
- Naturally curious and playful, can be very entertaining
- Produce high-quality fiber that can be spun into yarn or thread
- Also produce some milk which can be used
- Can be kept peacefully with other types of livestock, not just goats
- Display a variety of colors and patterns
- Can help to improve and trim pastures by eating the weeds and brush
- Not terribly expensive to raise and keep

Cons for Pygora Goats

- Require much more space than other typical pets
- Males and females can't be housed together unless the males are castrated
- Intact males may produce unpleasant odors, and can make a mess as well
- Require a fenced-in enclosure to contain them and keep predators away
- Have a tendency to escape if the enclosure isn't properly fenced
- Not recommended as solitary animals, require 2 or more to be happy

Chapter Four: Purchasing Pygora Goats

After reading the first few chapters of this book, you may have already come to the conclusion that a Pygora Goat is the right pet for you. If this is the case, you are ready to move on to learning where and how to purchase one. In this chapter, you will find information regarding where to purchase or rescue Pygora Goats in both the U.S. and the U.K. You will also learn how to identify a healthy Pygora Goat so you do not bring home an animal that is already sick.

1.) Where to Buy Pygora Goats

Now that you know that the Pygora Goat is the right choice for you, you can start thinking of where to buy one! Do not necessarily buy the first goat you come across --- not only do you need to determine that the goat comes from a good breeder, but also that it is healthy. In this section, you will learn where to look in buying or rescuing a Pygora Goat.

a.) Buying in the U.S.

In the United States you have a number of options for purchasing Pygora Goats. If you perform a simple online search you will find a number of farms specializing in the breeding of these animals. Before buying a goat, however, you should ensure that the breeder you are purchasing from is reputable. If you live in a rural area, ask around for referrals or get a recommendation from your veterinarian.

Try some of these websites for Pygora breeders:

PBA Breeders Directory. <http://www.pba-pygora.com/breederslisting.asp>

Pygora Goat Breeders Directory.
<http://www.goatfinder.com/pygora_goat_directory.htm>

Great Lakes Pygora. <http://www.greatlakespygora.com/>

Hawks Mountain Ranch Pygora Goats.
<http://www.hawksmtnranch.com/>

A less conventional option for obtaining a Pygora Goat may be to find a local goat rescue. Perform an online search or contact your local council regarding goat rescues in your area – you may also be able to obtain information from your local ASPCA shelter. Adopting a goat is an excellent option because the goat is likely already disbudded and neutered – it may also be a less expensive option than buying from a breeder.

Try one of these Pygora Goat rescues:

Puget Sound Goat Rescue. <http://www.goatsave.org/>

Hope Haven Farm Sanctuary. <http://hopehavenfarm.org/>

b.) Buying in the U.K.

If you are looking for a reputable Pygora Goat breeder, the first place you should look is the British Goat Society (BGS). The BGS provides its members with the opportunity to advertise on the website and may also be able to provide you with a list of breeders in your area. You may also want to ask your veterinarian if he knows of any reputable goat breeders.

Try some of these Pygora Goat breeders:

Well Manor Farm. <http://www.wellmanorfarm.co.uk/Southdown%20Fleece.html>

Hollyhock Hollow. <http://hhollow.com/>

Another option is to contact the Royal Society for the Prevention of Cruelty to Animals (RSPCA). The RSPCA runs animal shelters throughout the U.K. and they may have Pygora Goats in need of adoption. If you are looking for a pet goat and do not want to go through the hassle of weaning, disbudding and neutering a goat, you may want to consider adopting an adult goat.

Buttercups Sanctuary for Goats.
<http://www.buttercups.org.uk/rescues.html>

Preloved. <http://www.preloved.co.uk/adverts/list/3363/other-pets.html?keyword=pygmy%20goats>

Rainbow Valley Pony and Goat Sanctuary. <http://www.rainbowvalleysanctuary.org.uk/>

**Note: Purchasing animals online and having them shipped is typically considered animal cruelty. You have no control over the environment to which the animals are exposed or over the method of handling. Whenever possible, avoid purchasing animals online.

2.) *How to Select a Healthy Pygora Goat*

In addition to choosing a reputable breeder for your Pygora Goat, you also need to evaluate the goat itself – as well as its breeding stock. Before you purchase a goat, and certainly before you take it home, you need to be sure it is healthy. There is nothing worse than bringing home your new pet to find that it is sick – this can result in a lot of financial burden as well as the heartache of possibly losing your new pet to an untreatable illness.

When you go to look at the goat you are considering purchasing, look for some of these signs:

- Clear, bright eyes
- Sleek, glossy coat (no evidence of parasites)
- Clean under the tail (no evidence of diarrhea)
- No discharge coming from the nose or eyes
- Posture is strong and alert
- Feet are healthy and in good condition
- Goat is able to walk freely and easily
- Udder is spherical and free from lumps

It is also a good idea to speak to the breeder, asking a few questions about the goat in question as well as the breeding stock.

Some of the questions you might ask include:
- Does the goat have a healthy appetite?
- Has the goat been fully weaned? (If it is a kid)
- Are the goat's parents registered with the NPGA and AAGBA?
- What kind of diet has the goat been raised on?
- Do you offer any kind of health guarantee or documentation?
- Is the goat already registered or pre-registered?

If you can, you should also take a look around the property to make sure that the goats have been kept in clean, healthy conditions. If you are purchasing a kid, ask to see the parents so you can determine whether they are in good health or not – this will be an additional indicator of the health of the kid.

Chapter Five: Caring for Pygora Goats

Two of the most important things you must know before purchasing Pygora Goats is what will be required to create a healthy habitat and what to feed the goats. Offering your goats a healthy diet is the key to keeping them in good condition – you will need to keep a store of a variety of foods on hand so your goats get a well-balanced diet. In this chapter, you will learn the basics about creating the ideal habitat and diet for your Pygora Goats.

1.) Habitat Requirements

One of the most important elements in keeping Pygora Goats is providing a healthy habitat. For goats, this generally means a fenced-in area in which they can roam and graze. Additionally, you may need to provide a playground or other enrichment opportunities. In this section, you will learn everything you need to know about building a habitat for your Pygora Goats.

a.) Basic Habitat Needs

All Pygora Goats need in terms of habitat is space to roam, food to forage and shelter from the weather. There are three main areas that can be used for keeping Pygora Goats. The first option is to keep your goats in a large, fenced-off pasture. The pasture will give your goats space to run and play as well as food to forage. If you choose this option, you should be sure that there are no poisonous plants in the area and that it is secure from predators.

Another option is to take a small field and divide it into several portions using fencing. You can keep the goats in one area and, as they consume the foliage in that portion, move them to the next. This method is called rotational pasturing and it ensures that the foliage in one area is able to re-grow before the goats return.

For a small number of goats, a large yard may also be acceptable. The benefits of this option are that it is easily contained, parasites may not proliferate the soil as easily as in a pasture and the ground may be rough enough to help ground down the goats' hooves naturally. On the other hand, there is little food for your goats to forage so you will have to bring all of their food to them – you will also have to supply fresh water and an area where the goats can play and exercise.

b.) Providing Shelter

Goats generally do not like getting wet so it is important that you provide them with a shelter from rain. Your goats should have access to shelter at all times – either by leaving the main goat house accessible or by constructing temporary shelters in the enclosure. The main goat house should be a four-walled enclosure where you can keep your goats secured at night and during bad weather.

In both the main goat house and temporary shelters, you should provide plenty of soft bedding. The shelter itself should be large enough to accommodate all of your goats at one time. The ideal construction materials for a goat shelter include wood, stone, concrete or a mixture of these materials – metal is not a good material to use because it will get very hot in the summer and very cold during the winter. In regards to space, a goat shelter should provide at least 2 square meters (6 square feet) of floor space per goat.

The roof of the goat shelter needs to be leak-proof to keep out rain. You should also be sure to provide proper ventilation in the shelter without creating draughts. To make cleaning the shelter easier, the floor should be made of concrete and slightly sloped – after removing the bedding it can be easily washed clean. The ideal bedding for Pygora Goats is straw, though peat or wood shavings can also be used. The bedding should be mucked out and replaced about once a week, depending on the number of goats you keep.

c.) Fencing Materials

While having a shelter for your Pygora Goats is important, they will spend most of their time outside. It is important that you provide enough space for your goats to roam and exercise, but the area should be fenced off to keep the goats from escaping and to keep predators from getting in. Ideally, you should provide at least 8.5 square meters of outdoor space per goat – this will give them enough room to run without feeling confined.

In terms of the fence itself, it should be very strong and durable. Goats are excellent jumpers and climbers – though Pygora Goats may be small, they may surprise you in their abilities as escape artists. For this reason hedges and stone walls are not good options for fencing. To build an enclosure for goats, use strong wood or metal vertical posts that are driven well into the ground. For the fencing itself, use chain link or galvanized wire mesh with small enough apertures that your goats cannot fit their heads, legs or bodies through the gaps.

Warning: Electrical livestock fencing can be used for goats to provide additional protection from predators but you need to be very careful when installing it – you should also take care that your goats do not come into contact with the fence often. Barbed wire fences are never a good option for goats because they may try to jump over them, becoming tangled.

d.) Enrichment Opportunities

Pygora Goats have a natural curiosity and a playful demeanor. They love to climb and explore so they would enjoy the addition of a "playground" to their enclosure. A playground for these goats need not be extravagant – it can be made up of tree stumps, old tires, wooden benches and even scrap wood. Use your creativity to provide some enrichment for your goats by creating a playground for them to enjoy.

If you do not have the means to provide an entire playground for your goats, make the effort to provide a few simple enrichment opportunities. Pygora Goats love to hop onto hay bales or climb up trees – they may even use abandoned farm equipment as a playground! Another option is to provide your goat with a few empty buckets that they can toss around.

e.) Keeping Goats in Urban Areas

Recently, there has been a movement toward re-establishing the principles of homesteading. Homesteading simply means becoming more self-sufficient whether by growing your own food or producing your own textiles.

Keeping Pygora Goats is a great option for homesteaders because they produce high-quality wool that can be used for clothing as well as small amounts of milk that can be used to make into cheese.

Homesteading is becoming increasingly popular in urban areas where people want to make an effort to reconnect with nature and reduce their carbon footprint. Keeping livestock in urban areas can be a challenge but, because Pygora Goats are small, it can be done. Keep these elements in mind when considering keeping Pygora Goats in an urban environment:

- You will need to check the zoning regulations and requirements for your area to see whether it is legal to keep goats and if you need a particularly license to do so.

- Excellent fencing is needed to keep your goats contained and to protect them from dogs and other people.

- Make sure you have enough space to provide your goat with adequate room for roaming, grazing and shelter.

- Remember that goats are social animals and are best kept in pairs or groups – check local legislation to make sure there isn't a cap on the number of goats you can keep.

- Check with your neighbors before you get the goats – the last thing you want is to cause problems that may lead to you losing the goat down the line.

- Be sure you have enough time to dedicate to feeding and caring for your goats, especially if you have a full-time job.

Pygora Goats are typically hardy animals, able to adapt to a variety of situations. Just because they may be able to survive in an environment that is less than ideal, however, doesn't mean that they should have to. If you are considering keeping goats in an urban environment, make sure you can meet the basic needs of your goats before you actually purchase any.

2.) Feeding Pygora Goats

The most important aspect of keeping your Pygora Goats healthy involves providing them with a well-balanced diet. Pygora Goats are herbivores which means that their diet is entirely composed of vegetation. You can't simply give your goat a pile of vegetables and expect him to be healthy, however – these goats have specific nutritional needs. You will learn about these needs in this section.

a.) Nutritional Needs

Pygora Goats require constant access to fresh, clean water. Goats do tend to be fairly messy, so you may need to check their water several times a day and refresh it if necessary. You should be careful about where you place water troughs and buckets so the goats do not accidentally urinate or defecate in them – if they do, the water should be changed immediately. Generally, goats prefer water that is slightly warm. A single goat can consume 4 to 6 gallons (18 to 27 liters) of water a day.

In addition to fresh water, your goats need a supply of fresh hay. Pygora Goats are ruminant animals which means their stomachs have several compartments, one of which is designed to soften fibrous plant food. The first compartment of the stomach is called the rumen and it contains bacteria that helps to break down plant material. The plant material is then regurgitated and then chewed again to break it down further for digestion.

Fibrous foods such as hay should make up about 50% of a goat's diet. This hay should be fresh and free from signs of mold – a 40-pound (18 kg) bale of hay will last a single Pygora Goat about one month. Aside from hay, another 25% of your goat's diet should be made up of extra vegetation such as grass, roots, branches and other non-toxic plant foods. In order for a goat's rumen to work properly, they need to eat long, fibrous foods – thus, when giving your goat grass or hay, it should be at least 4 inches (10 cm.) long.

In addition to fresh hay, you may want to round out your Pygora Goats' diet with additional plant material or concentrates. Concentrates are a type of commercial food, often in the form of pellets, which provide goats with additional vitamins and minerals. When feeding your goats concentrates it is essential that you also provide plenty of long hay or grass so they can properly digest the concentrates.

Note: An adult goat does not need a lot of concentrate in its diet – feeding too much can lead to obesity and, in males, the development of urinary tract issues such as bladder stones.

b.) Tips for Feeding

Like many goats, Pygora Goats prefer not to eat food that has touched the floor. For this reason, you will need to purchase a number of hayracks. Hayracks can be found at most feed stores and farm supply stores – they can be covered with a lid to keep the hay in and should be positioned at such a height that your goats will not accidentally soil the hay inside. If you have multiple goats, you will need to buy a hayrack large enough that all of the goats can feed at once without competing for space.

Because goats have very sensitive stomachs, it is important that you make any changes to their diet gradually. These goats do appreciate variety in their diet but sudden changes in dietary routine could cause digestive issues. Goats rely on the bacteria in their rumen to help digest their food – if you introduce new foods suddenly, the bacteria will not be able to digest it right away. Rather, introduce small amounts of new food so the bacteria in your goats' stomachs can adjust.

Caution: Never use hay nets for goats – these are intended for horses and Pygora Goats can easily become entangled in the nets.

c.) Supplemental Food Sources

Many Pygora Goat owners choose to let their goats wander free in pasture areas. The plants in this area will serve as a supplemental food source for your goats, helping to round out their diet.

Some of the edible foods that may be found in pasture areas for goats include:

Acorns	Dogwood	Mesquite
Bamboo	Elm	Mint
Beets	English Ivy	Morning Glory
Blackberry Bushes	Fern	Onion
Black Locus	Ficus	Pepper Plants
Bramble	Garlic	Poison Ivy/Oak
Camellias	Ginger	Poplar Trees
Collard Greens	Grape Vines	Raspberry Bushes
Cedar	Greenbrier	Rose Bushes
Clover	Hibiscus	Spruce Trees
Comfrey	Hyssop	Sunflowers
Corn Husks	Ivy	Tomato Plants
Cottonwood	Lilac	Virginia Creeper
Dandelion	Lupine	Weeping Willow
Douglas Fir	Maple Trees	

**Note: This is not a complete listing of plants that are edible for goats. For additional information, see: <http://fiascofarm.com/goats/poisonousplants.htm>

Because Pygora Goats may not automatically avoid toxic plants, you need to be very careful about what plants to keep on your property. Many wild plants including weeds and grasses are edible for goats but some are extremely toxic and could kill your goats if they ingest it.

Some of the most important plants to avoid include:

Alder	Evergreen Shrubs	Hemlock
Laurel	Tulips	Ragwort
Privet	Daffodils	Nightshades
Rhododendron	Foxglove	Bryony
Yew	Mayweed	Laburnum
Honeysuckle	Celandine	Delphinium
Walnut	Buttercup	

3.) Shearing Pygora Goats

As you have already learned, Pygora Goats are capable of producing three different types of fleece. Goats with fiber Types B and C typically shed their coats so, if you do not plan to harvest the fleece, you do not need to shear them. Goats with Type A coats do not blow their coats, however, so shearing is necessary.

Most goat owners shear their goats in the spring before kidding season. The soft undercoat tends to grow thicker during the winter to provide insulation for the goat so, by the spring, it should be long enough to shear.

Shearing Pygora Goats isn't necessarily difficult, but it does require a certain amount of time and preparation. Before shearing, you must prepare the coat to remove fleas and ticks. After shearing, you then need to sort the fiber, separating out the guard hairs. Once the fleece has been prepared you can move on to spinning it for use.

Follow the steps listed below to shear your Pygora Goats:

1. Consider treating your goats with a topical insecticide like pyrethrin or permethrin to kill any lice or ticks – do this two to three weeks before shearing.

2. Keep the goats inside for 24 hours before shearing to ensure that their coats are dry.

3. Gather the necessary supplies – this includes your sheep shears, scissors, grooming stand or stanchion, blow drier and a bag for collecting the fiber.

4. Secure your Pygora Goat to the stanchion or grooming stand and blow the coat to remove any hay or other debris.

5. If your goat's coat has any mud on it, wash this out before shearing to avoid driving it deeper into the fiber.

6. Use the shears to shear the goat's belly first – move the shears in long, smooth strokes.

7. Shear the goat's sides, working from the belly up to the spine from the back leg to the front leg on each side.

8. Start at the base of the goat's throat and move upward to shear the neck, working up the chest toward the ears.

9. Trim any excess hair with scissors.

10. Release your goat into a clean and dry area with fresh bedding – plan to keep them out of the cold and wet for at least a month.

11. Sort through the fiber by hand and remove any soiled fleece and contaminants like hay.

12. Roll the clean fleece up in a bag and store it in a cool and dry area until you are ready to prepare it for spinning.

Shearing is something that takes time to learn and, with practice, you will become better at it. If you have several goats, start with the youngest goats first and end with the oldest. Older goats tend to have coarser fiber so you want to keep it from mixing with the finer wool. While you are still learning how to shear properly, consider practicing on the goats with lower quality fiber. Hopefully you will have the hang of it by the time you are ready to shear the goats with the highest quality fiber.

**Note: For information about preparing and spinning Pygora Goat fiber, refer to Chapter Seven: Uses for Pygora Goats.

Chapter Six: Breeding Pygora Goats

Breeding Pygora Goats can be a wonderful experience, but it is not something you should do on a whim. It takes time, planning and patience in order to breed Pygora Goats properly and to raise happy and healthy kids. In this chapter, you will learn the basics about how Pygora Goats breed as well as some tips for breeding your own Pygora Goats at home.

1.) Basic Breeding Info

For the most part, breeding Pygora Goats is not difficult – goats are eager to breed anyway. What can be challenging, however, is arranging and overseeing the breeding process to ensure that your female goat remains healthy throughout the pregnancy and that you raise the kids properly. Before you can think about breeding your goats, you need to learn how the process works and what you can expect.

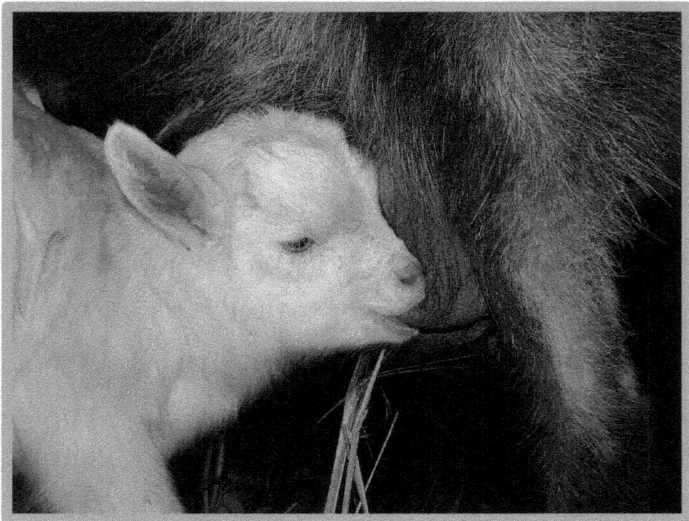

Pygora Goats can technically be bred all year round, but it is generally recommended that you only breed a doe once per year at most. The normal breeding season for these goats is between July and February, so try to make your breeding plans accordingly. Pygora Goats are capable of birthing one to four kids at a time, though they commonly have twins. The gestation period for these goats is between 140 and 150 days.

Female goats typically go into heat (estrus) every 18 to 21 days and the estrus cycle itself lasts 2 to 3 days. This is the ideal time for breeding because it ensures the greatest likelihood of conception. Once conception has occurred, the gestation period begins and lasts up to 150 days. At birth, Pygora Goat kids typically weigh about 5 lbs. (2.2 kg.) but they grow very quickly. Female goats are very good at raising their kids and most are naturally weaned before they reach 12 weeks of age.

2.) The Breeding Process

In order to breed your Pygora Goats successfully, you need to not only know the basics of their breeding info, but also how to plan for it. This involves tracking and understanding the heat cycles of your does and arranging multiple couplings to ensure conception. You should also learn what to expect while your doe is pregnant and what you can do to prepare for the kids.

To ensure the greatest chance of a successful mating, it is best to attempt breeding when the doe is in heat. One of the signs of heat is a mucus discharge coming from the vulva of the female, resulting in matted hair around the tail. Other signs include frequent urination, loss of appetite and bleating. When the doe is ready for breeding, it is best to introduce the doe to the buck – take the female to the male instead of the other way around. Many goat breeders recommend two to four breeding sessions per estrus cycle to ensure conception.

Mature bucks can be mated many times a year. For bucks only one or two years old, it is recommended that you limit them to 25 services per year. Older bucks, however, can do up to 75 doe services a year. When you are ready to breed your Pygora Goats, record the date of the mating so you can predict the birth of the kids. This is important because, if the kidding becomes difficult for the doe, you should be around to help.

Summary of Facts

Does

Sexual Maturity: 8 to 12 months
Ideal Breeding Age: 1 year
Breeding Weight: 60% to 75% of adult weight
Estrus: 18 to 22 days
Length of Cycle: 2 to 3 days
Signs of Heat: bleating, frequent urination, lack of appetite
Gestation Period: 145 to 150 days
Number of Kids: one to four, often twins
Size of Newborns: 5 lbs. (2.2 kg.)

Bucks

Sexual Maturity: 8 to 12 months (may become fertile as early as 8 weeks of age)
Ideal Breeding Age: 8 to 10 months
Breeding Season: July through February
Breeding Ratio: 1 buck per 25 does

3.) Raising the Babies

It can sometimes be difficult to tell when a pregnant doe is about to give birth – this is why it is important to track the gestation period so you know when to expect it. There are a few signs you can look for when it comes near the end of the gestation period:

- The ligaments at the head of the tail may appear to disappear – go slack

- The tail head is noticeably raised

- The doe's udder is full and tight – it may also be glossy in appearance

- A mucus discharge coming from the doe's vagina – it will turn amber when kidding is imminent

- The doe may become more vocal – may also stretch and yawn

- Doe may exhibit unusual behavior or become more affectionate

In most cases, a doe is able to handle the kidding herself but it is a good idea for you to be nearby in case there is a problem. Once the kids are born, the mother will clean them and encourage them to nurse. After the kids are born, it is important that they suckle from their mother as soon as possible. The first milk produced after birth is called colostrum and it contains high quantities of antibodies, vitamins and minerals that are essential for newborn kids.

If the doe is healthy, she should raise the kids well enough on her own and you won't have to do much yourself aside from providing food and general care. It is okay to let the kids nurse for as long as they like because they will likely wean themselves before they reach 3 months of age. Pygora Goat kids may begin grazing as early as 2 weeks of age and will eventually start consuming more solid food and less milk from their dam. Weaning can be stressful on kids, so it is important to keep a close eye on them during this period.

Chapter Seven: Uses for Pygora Goats

Though Pygora Goats are often kept as pets, there are a number of other benefits to owning them. Their beautiful fiber, for example, can be spun into homemade wool and used for yarn and clothing. Most domestic goats can also be used for brush control and some can even be milked. In this chapter, you will learn about the various purposes Pygora Goats are able to serve and how to take advantage of these benefits yourself.

1.) Fiber Production

Before you can spin the fiber produced by your Pygora Goat, you need to understand its components. These goats produce both guard hair and soft fiber. In order to spin the fiber, you need to first remove the guard hairs. The amount of guard hairs any given Pygora Goat produces greatly depends on the type of fiber. Type A goats, for example, do not produce many guard hairs so the fiber can often be used "as is". Type C goats, however, must be de-haired because the guard hairs are very coarse.

a.) Preparing the Fiber

When it comes to preparing Pygora Goat fiber for spinning, the methods vary depending on the type of Fiber. Type A, for example, must be shorn. Generally, this type of fleece does not have any guard hairs but you may want to brush the shorn fiber through with a comb or hand carder to remove any guard hairs. The fiber can then be spun directly from the shorn locks with no additional preparation needed.

Type B fiber is shorter and has more guard hairs than Type A. This being the case, plucking is the preferred method for harvesting this type of fiber rather than shearing. To pluck your goat's coat, all you have to do is run your hand through it and gently pull out the fibers that are ready to be shed. If the fibers do not release easily, wait a few days before trying again. Keep in mind that you may need to pluck your goat in stages, repeating the process every few days until finished.

With Type C fiber, either plucking or combing works well. Combing is essential the same method as plucking, you simply use a comb rather than your hands to pull the fiber free. These two methods limit the number of guard hairs in the final product. If you end up shearing a Type B or Type C goat, you will need to de-hair the fiber using a mini-comb. Unfortunately, this method results in a fairly low yield and it must be done very gently to avoid breaking the fibers in the process.

b.) Spinning the Fiber

Pygora Goat fiber tends to be very soft and slippery, so you need to be careful how to spin it. In order to keep the yarn together, you will need to twist it well enough for it to hold. Maintaining a smooth rhythm during spinning will also help to improve the quality of the finished product. It is important to note that certain types of fiber should be spun in certain ways – Type A should be spun thin, Type B can be spun a bit thicker, but Type C shouldn't be spun too thick because the yarn is so warm on its own.

The two most popular methods for spinning Pygora yarn are using a hand spindle or a spinning wheel. Getting used to a spinning wheel can be challenging so, when you are still getting used to the quality of your Pygora's fiber, you may want to start out using a drop spindle.

To use a drop spindle, follow these instructions:

1. Stand up straight and hole the leader thread of the spindle in the hand you intend to hold the fiber with (this is your fiber hand), letting the spindle itself hang free.

2. Practice spinning the spindle a few times, twisting it with your fingers so it turns to the right.

3. Gather your fiber and tuck it under your arm or wrap it loosely around your wrist, bringing the end of it through the palm of your hand.

4. Overlap the end of the fiber with about 10 inches of the leader thread and hold it in place by pinching it loosely between your thumb and forefinger on your fiber hand.

5. Give the spindle a firm twist to the right – as the leader thread twists, the fiber should begin to twist as well.

6. Pinch your thumb and forefinger tighter on the leader and fiber, bringing both closer to the spindle to tighten the yarn.

7. Once you have about 3 inches of tightly spun yarn on the leader, relax your fingers and move them down the leader and fiber, letting the twist spread.

8. Alternate between tightening your grip on your fiber hand and your spinning hand, slowly transferring the twist along the stretched fiber.

Follow these instructions to use a spinning wheel:

1. Sit down at the wheel with the end of your fiber gathered in one hand (this is your fiber hand – the other is your spinning hand).

2. Lay the leader over the fiber and spin the wheel gently to the right while pushing down on the treadle.

3. Pinch the leader and fiber together with your spinning hand and pull it forward about 3 inches to tighten the yarn.

4. Slide the pinched fingers of your spinning hand slowly back toward your fiber hand, letting the twist from the leader move into the fiber.

5. Repeat the process, alternating the movement of your spinning hand and your fiber hand, working the twist through the length of fiber.

6. When you run out of fiber, simply add another length using the same method described in Step 2.

c.) Fluffing the Yarn

Once you have a completed skein of Pygora yarn, soak it in hot water for a few minutes. Squeeze out as much water as possible then soak in it ice water for a few minutes. Squeeze out the cold water and repeat the process two or three more times. After ringing out the yarn, smack it on a clean surface several times until the yarn begins to fluff up. Let the fluffed yarn dry and, if necessary, repeat the entire process.

**Note: Everyone has their own preferences for the thickness and fluffiness of Pygora yarn. As you get the hang of spinning, you will learn how you like it and you will settle into a rhythm and habit for preparing your Pygora's fiber.

2.) Brush-Eaters

Though fiber production is the primary reason most people keep Pygora Goats, they can serve a secondary purpose as a means of brush control. Goats are often referred to as "natural lawnmowers" because they are not picky about what they eat, consuming grass, weeds and other plants without discrimination. If you have a significant amount of property and choose to use that land as a pasture for your goats, they will help to keep it trimmed.

You should realize, of course, that using goats for brush control is not as reliable or consistent as mowing or trimming the brush yourself. While goats may help to keep weeds and brush from growing out of control, the brush will certainly not look as uniform or well-manicured as it might if you did it yourself. Goats are also likely to leave certain patches or spindly stalks untouched, for whatever reason, which could spread seed and repopulate the area with weeds and other problem plants.

It is also important to note that providing your Pygora Goats with a pasture in which to graze should not be considered an alternative to offering them hay. In order to keep your goats healthy, you need to provide them with a balanced diet and they may not get all the nutrients they need from brush alone. Weeds, grass and brush should be considered a source of supplemental nutrition only.

Though there are some disadvantages to using Pygora Goats for brush control, there are benefits as well. If you are not particular about keeping the lawn neatly trimmed, letting your goats graze on the lawn can help to keep the weeds and brush trimmed back to some degree. Pygora Goats, like all goats, tend to make a bit of a mess but you can use their droppings and wasted hay to get a good-sized compost pile started. Leaving your goats out to pasture also gives them good opportunities for exercise and enrichment, both of which are essential for keeping your goats healthy.

3.) Milk Producers

While Pygora Goats aren't traditionally bred for their milk, they do produce it. Pygora Goat does are capable of producing between one and four kids, though twins is typical. In order to care for their young, they must produce enough for their kids to nurse. Because these goats are not bred for milking, however, their udders and teats tend to be very small. This makes the task of milking difficult and, according to many Pygora owners, not worth the effort.

If you intend to milk your Pygora Goats, it would be best to invest in a milker. These devices come in a range of sizes and can be designed for animals with small teats – you will need to measure your Pygora Goat and choose a milker of the appropriate size. You should also keep in mind that not all goats willingly submit to the milking process – if they haven't been handled enough, they may be too skittish and could be frightened of the machine.

4.) Kid-Friendly Pets

Pygora Goats are known for being friendly, but energetic animals and they make very entertaining pets. Because they are fairly small in size and generally good with people, Pygora Goats are considered to be kid-friendly pets. It is important to realize, however, that caring for a goat requires a great deal of responsibility. Not all children are old enough or responsible enough to handle the challenge.

Before purchasing a Pygora Goat as a pet for your child, have a discussion with your child to make sure they understand the responsibilities involved. Not only will they have to feed the goat on a daily basis, but they will also have to clean up after it and, depending on the fiber type, care for its coat. For many people, owning goats is a family affair but it is important for your children to understand that they will be expected to take part in the care of their new pet.

Chapter Eight: Keeping Pygora Goats Healthy

Keeping Pygora Goats, or any other pet, is a big responsibility. As a pet owner, it is your duty to provide your goats with the proper care and healthy environment they need in order to thrive. In addition to providing for the basic needs of your goats, you should also take preventive measures against disease. In this chapter, you will learn the basics about common conditions affecting Pygora Goats so you can identify and treat them properly. You will also learn some tips for preventing disease.

1.) Common Health Problems

As long as you keep your Pygora Goats in a clean environment and provide access to good food and water, you shouldn't have to worry about too many serious diseases. It is possible, however, for domestic goats like Pygora Goats to become ill at one time or another. In order to prepare yourself for this possibility, take the time to read up on some of the conditions commonly affecting this breed so you will be ready to identify and treat them, if needed.

The following conditions are fairly common in domestic goats including Pygora Goats:

- Coccidiosis
- Enterotoxemia
- External Parasites
- Footrot
- Internal Parasites
- Keratoconjunctivitis
- Lameness
- Mastitis
- Respiratory Problems
- Scours
- Soremouth

Coccidiosis

This condition is caused by protozoan parasites called *Coccidia*. This parasites can cause damage to the lining of the small intestine which often results in the malabsorption of nutrients and thus weight loss, stunted growth and/or diarrhea. Other symptoms of Coccidiosis include fever, anemia, dehydration, and secondary infections.

This condition tends to infect goats that are kept in close quarters or in unsanitary conditions – kids between the age of one and six months are at the greatest risk. Spread of the disease can be controlled through increased sanitation efforts and through treatment with sulfa drugs.

Cause: protozoan parasites, *Coccidia*
Symptoms: dehydration, anemia, weight loss, diarrhea, stunted growth
Treatment: increased sanitation efforts and sulfa drugs

Enterotoxemia

Also known as overeating disease, enterotoxemia may manifest in several forms. This condition is almost always associated with a change in diet or a change in the quality of the feed used. Symptoms of the disease may include fever, watery diarrhea, decreased milk yield and death. If not treated within 48 hours, the condition is often fatal. Treatment for enterotoxemia may include antitoxins and antibiotics.

Cause: change in diet or change in feed quality
Symptoms: fever, watery diarrhea, decreased milk yield
Treatment: antitoxins and antibiotics

External Parasites

External parasite infections often manifest in the form of skin problems. Some of the most common external parasites are lice and mites. These infections are most common during winter when Pygora Goats are kept indoors in close quarters. Various parasites affect goats in different ways. Chewing lice, for example, feed on dead skin cells while sucking lice feed on the animal's blood. Mites burrow into the skin, causing itching, skin irritation, hair loss and scabs or lesions. Treatment may include topical insecticides or injectable Ivermectin.

Cause: lice and mites
Symptoms: itching, skin irritation, hair loss and scabs or lesions
Treatment: topical insecticides or injectable Ivermectin.

Footrot

Also called foot scald, footrot is a bacterial infection affecting the foot of goats. This infection is caused by either *Fusobacterium necrophorum* or *Dichelobacter nodus* and it is most common in warm, most areas. In virulent cases, the bacteria actually enter the hoof, digesting the horny sole and eating into the fleshy tissue. Common symptoms of this disease include redness of the toes, inflammation and bad odor. In extreme cases, the horn of the hoof may actually separate from the hoof wall. If left untreated, footrot can lead to lameness, weight loss and decreased reproductive capabilities.

This condition is often introduced when a new goat is brought into the herd. Goats are more at risk for this condition when their hooves are not trimmed regularly and when they are kept in crowded conditions. Treatment options include foot soaking baths of zinc sulfate, vaccination and antibiotic treatments.

Cause: *Fusobacterium necrophorum* or *Dichelobacter nodus* bacteria
Symptoms: redness of the toes, inflammation and bad odor
Treatment: foot soaking baths of zinc sulfate, vaccination and antibiotic treatments.

Internal Parasites

Pygora Goats can be affected by a number of internal parasites including roundworms, tapeworms, lungworms, coccidia and nematodes. Common symptoms of internal parasite infections include diarrhea, weight loss, loss of appetite and reduced growth rates. Roundworms are the most common type of parasite affecting goats – these infections often cause anemia, edema, weakness and lethargy.

Tapeworms tend to infect the digestive tract and may result in yellowish-white stools. Tapeworm infections are most common in kids under four months of age because kids quickly develop a resistance to them. Treatment for internal parasite infections vary from one disease to another but de-worming medications are the most common.

Cause: roundworms, tapeworms, lungworms, coccidia and nematodes
Symptoms: diarrhea, weight loss, loss of appetite and reduced growth rates
Treatment: de-worming medications

Keratoconjunctivitis

Pinkeye, or infectious keratoconjunctivitis, is most likely to occur during warm weather. This disease is highly contagious and can easily be spread through close contact or by flies. Stress is a significant factor in the spread of this disease as are good sanitation and fly control. Common signs of the disease include redness of the eye, swelling or excess tearing – if the disease progresses, it may also result in opacity of the eye, corneal ulcers and blindness. Treatment for this disease typically involves broad-spectrum antibiotics.

Cause: spread through close contact or flies
Symptoms: redness of the eye, swelling, excess tearing
Treatment: broad-spectrum antibiotics

Lameness

Lameness occurs when a goat is no longer able to use one or more of its limbs. This condition is often caused by compaction of debris between the toes, injury to the legs or feet, bacterial infection of the feet, footrot or penetration of the feet by thorns or stones.

If a Pygora Goat begins to limp or becomes reluctant to stand up or move around, it should immediately be separated from the other goats. The affected goat should be isolated, kept on dry straw and undergo inspection of the legs and feet. Treatment depends on the cause of the condition and generally must be determined by a veterinarian.

Cause: compaction of debris between the toes, injury to the legs or feet, bacterial infection of the feet, footrot or penetration of the feet by thorns or stones

Symptoms: limping, favoring one leg, reluctance to stand up or move around

Treatment: depends on the cause of the condition

Mastitis

Mastitis is a bacterial infection of the mammary gland resulting in inflammation. One of the leading causes for the culling of goats and other livestock is udder damage resulting from mastitis. Symptoms of this condition include warm or swollen mammary glands, milk of abnormal color or consistency and depression. If the bacteria enter the bloodstream, the infected goat may become septic and exhibit additional symptoms such as anorexia, fever, depression and lethargy.

Though technically caused by bacteria, the risk for this disease increases with poor sanitation. A systemic infection or trauma inflicted upon the udder may also contribute to development of the disease. Treatment for mastitis often involves intra-mammary and system antibiotic treatment. In some cases, udder damage may occur despite treatment.

Cause: bacterial infection of the mammary gland resulting in inflammation
Symptoms: warm or swollen mammary glands, milk of abnormal color or consistency and depression
Treatment: intra-mammary and system antibiotic treatment

Respiratory Problems

Respiratory problems like pneumonia are most common in kids, but they can affect goats of any age. There are many different kinds of respiratory problems but they are most often caused by some combination of bacterial and viral agents infecting the lungs. These problems are more likely to occur in goats that are already stressed due to weaning, poor air quality, transport or a change in weather.

The most common signs of pneumonia include fever, moist cough and difficulty breathing – depression and loss of appetite may also occur. Treatment for pneumonia typically involves the administration of antibiotics but it may depend on the diagnosis. The disease can be prevented by keeping goats in dry, well-ventilated areas and by minimizing the stress to which they are exposed.

Cause: combination of viral and bacterial agents infecting the lungs; often brought on by stress
Symptoms: fever, wet cough, difficulty breathing, loss of appetite, depression
Treatment: depends on diagnosis; often antibiotics

Scours

Scours is a term used to refer to diarrheal diseases, particularly those most common in kids. These diseases are often caused by coccidia, worms, salmonella and various viruses. The symptoms of the disease vary but often include anorexia, fever, weakness and watery stools. Treatment for this condition includes antibiotics, intestinal astringents and fluid therapy. Preventive measures for scours involve good sanitation and proper housing.

Cause: coccidia, worms, salmonella and various viruses
Symptoms: anorexia, fever, weakness and watery stools

Treatment: antibiotics, intestinal astringents and fluid therapy

Soremouth

Also called contagious ecthyma, soremouth is a type of viral skin disease. This disease is caused by a virus which enters the body through broken skin and results in infection of the mouth, nose, udder or teats. Symptoms of the disease include scabs or blisters, loss of condition, stunted growth and loss of appetite. When this condition affects the teats of lactating does it can be very harmful because it becomes painful for the doe to nurse her kids – this may result in premature weaning. In some cases, the disease will go away on its own but it can also be treated with an iodine/glycerin solution.

Cause: a virus which enters the body through broken skin
Symptoms: scabs or blisters, loss of condition, stunted growth and loss of appetite
Treatment: treatment with iodine/glycerin solution

2.) Preventing Illness

Vaccinating Pygora Goats is not quite the same as it is for cats and dogs, but it is equally important. By vaccinating your goats, you can help to prepare their bodies for future contact with the disease so they do not get sick.

Vaccinations are the primary method of disease prevention among livestock like the Pygora Goats, in addition to general hygiene and cleanliness.

Though other vaccinations may be recommended by your veterinarian according to the risk level for the area in which you live, the only vaccine that is universally recommended for goats is against clostridial diseases. This vaccine is not required by law, but it is a good idea to vaccinate your whole herd to protect them against this illness. After the first vaccination, plan to administer a booster shot to each of your goats every 4 to 6 months thereafter. Another disease which some goat owners vaccinate against is sore mouth, but vaccination is typically not necessary unless the goat has already been exposed to the disease.

In addition to vaccinating your goats properly, you should also have information for a local vet on hand. Not all veterinarians are qualified to care for livestock like goats, so take the time to research and find one who is. You may not need to take your goats in for regular check-ups, but it is a good idea to have the information on hand in case an emergency arises and your goats need veterinary care. If you do have your goats regularly checked by a vet, he or she will be able to recommend other vaccines that your goats could benefit from.

a.) Creating a Medical Kit

You never know when your goat might injure himself or fall ill. In cases like this, you will be glad to have a medical kit on hand. Below you will find a list of items to include in your goat medical kit – these are items that you will need to clean and sterilize wounds, to treat basic illnesses and to administer medications.

- Antihistamine (for insect bites)
- Aspirin
- Baking Soda
- Betadyne
- Bleach
- Blood Stopper (styptic powder)
- Cotton Balls
- Cotton Swabs

- Oral Electrolyte
- Epinephrine
- Terramycin (eye ointment)
- Feeding Tubes
- Hoof Trimmer
- Hydrogen Peroxide
- Iodine
- Ivermectin
- Milk of Magnesia
- Pepto Bismol (for diarrhea)
- Rubber Gloves
- Rubbing Alcohol
- Scissors
- Sheeting Strips (wound binding)
- Stethoscope
- Suture Needles
- Thermometer
- Tongue Depressors
- Tweezers
- Vaseline

Note: Remember, while it is good to have these things on hand for small wounds, it is always best to seek veterinary care for major injuries and bleeding wounds.

Chapter Nine: Showing Pygora Goats

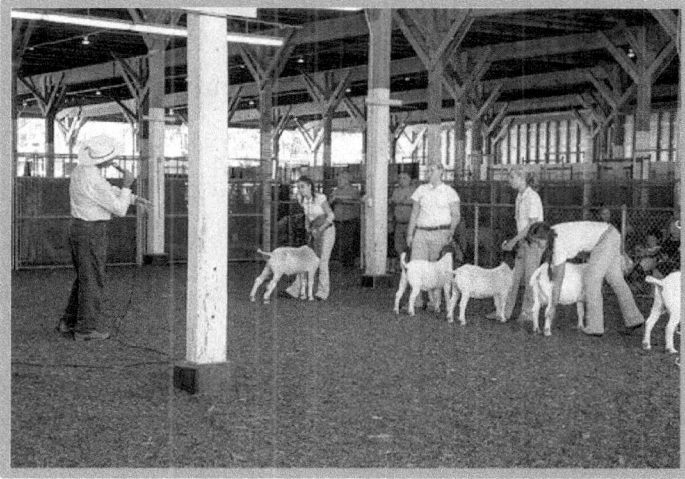

Showing your Pygora Goats can be an interesting challenge as well as a bonding experience for you and your pets. Goat shows are a great way to get to know other Pygora owners and breeders in your area – you may also pick up some tips for caring for your own goats. In this chapter, you will learn the basics about showing Pygora Goats including the breed standard and some tips for showing goats in general.

1.) Breed Standard

Before you show your Pygora Goats, you must make sure that they meet the Pygora Breeders Association (PBA) breed standards. This association sets forth guidelines for the breeding of Pygora Goats so that all specimens meet the standards of the breed – these standards are then used to evaluate goats in show and points are awarded based on how close the animals comes to meeting the breed standard.

According to the PBA, crossing an Angora Goat registered with the American Angora Goat Breeders Association (AAGBA) with a Pygmy Goat registered with the National Pygmy Goat Association (NPGA), creates a first-generation Pygora. On their registration papers, these goats are labeled F-1. It isn't until the second generation that a goat can be considered a true Pygora – it can contain no more than 75% of either Angora or Pygmy ancestry.

a.) Basics of the Breed Standard

According to the PBA breed standard, the Pygora is a medium-sized fleece goat with a well-muscled and balanced look. The goat should be about as long as it is tall. For females, the minimum size at 24 months is 18 inches (48 cm.) with the average being about 22 inches (56 cm.) For males, the minimum size is 23 inches (58 cm.) at 30 months with the average being about 27 inches (68.5 cm.). There is no limit for the maximize size according to the Pygora breed standard.

b.) Acceptable Colors and Patterns

Pygora goat kids are often born white, though they may develop a variety of colors and patterns as they age. The patterns described in the PBA standards include: white pattern, black pattern, agouti pattern and caramel pattern.

White Pattern: All white with no other color

Black Pattern: Solid black with black or dark-colored portions on the muzzle, forehead, eyes and ears. All black Pygoras have solid black stockings.

Agouti Pattern: All agouti Pygoras have dark solid-colored stockings with a lighter body color and lighter coloring in the muzzle, forehead, eyes and ears. Other colors may include: light grey, medium grey, dark grey, black, light brown, medium brown and dark brown.

Caramel Pattern: All Pygoras with caramel pattern have light vertical stripes on the front side of dark-colored stockings. The muzzle, forehead, eyes and ears are lighter than the rest of the body. Caramel colors may be light, medium, dark or brown.

c.) Pygora Goat Fleece

Type A: Long, lustrous fiber averaging 6 inches (15 cm.) in length; drapes in long ringlets. A single coat with no guard hair. Fiber is very fine (like mohair), less than 28 microns. Smooth and silky, cool to the touch.

Type B: Fiber with a blend of characteristics from Type A and Type C fibers. Generally curly, about 3 to 6 inches (7.6 to 15 cm.) in length. Should have a luster with obvious guard hair. Fiber is soft and airy, generally less than 24 microns.

Type C: Very fine fiber, similar to cashmere; generally below 18.5 microns. At least 1 inch (2.5 cm) long, usually between 1 and 3 inches (2.5 to 7.6 cm.). Matte finish with a crimp, coarse guard hair is present.

d.) Structure of Pygoras

Below you will find a breakdown of the different aspects of a Pygora's structure, according to the PBA standard.

Head and Neck: Medium-sized head with dished profile. Eyes wide-set, any color. Ears medium-long and drooping or erect. Nose wide and flat, bite even. Neck long and graceful, well-muscled.

Shoulder and Back: Shoulder closely attached to the withers. Back slopes slightly down from the withers, level along the chine and loin. Withers are sharp and obvious.

Loin, Rump and Hips: Loin broad and level, wide and pronounced. Rump is long, sloping about 30 degrees. Hips are wide but proportional, rectangular from rear view.

Legs and Feet: Forelegs are straight under shoulders, muscular without being cobby. Hind legs are set wide apart, straight down from the hips. Thighs are muscular, allowing for smooth movement. Feet are strong and symmetrical; hooves together with a level sole.

Barrel and Chest: Barrel is large and full. Body is pear-shaped when viewed from above. Ribs are well sprung with increasing space from head to tail. Chest is full and obvious, prosternum ahead of the shoulders.

e.) Other Points

Personality: Pygora goats should be alert and curious; friendly and easy to handle.

Reproductive System (Does): Capable of producing and feeding 1 to 4 kids; gestation period 145 to 150 days. Normal vaginal deliveries are desirable.

Reproductive System (Bucks): Two descended testicles; large, symmetrical and firm. The mature buck must be fertile.

2.) *What to Know Before Showing*

Before showing your Pygora Goats, the main thing you need to know is that your goats meet the PBA standards. In addition to the information provided in the previous section, you can find more details on the Pygora breed standard on the PBA website:

<http://www.pygoragoats.org/acrobat/Breed_Standard.pdf>

You may also find the following tips helpful in preparing for your first show:

- Practice walking with your goat before the show – you want to get your goat used to walking on a lead. This may also help to offset some nerves when the goat is walking in an unfamiliar show ring.

- Clean your goat well for the show – buy a new color and trim his hooves so they look clean.

- Always keep the goat between the judge and yourself – the judge is looking at the goat, so make sure he is always in full view.

- Stay calm. Even if your goat starts to misbehave, never hit it or treat it roughly.

- Always do what the judge asks – sometimes a judge will ask you to walk your goat in a line or ask you questions about the goat. Be sure you are always paying attention!

- Don't talk to your neighbor, especially while the judge is examining your goat or your neighbor's goat – it is considered very rude.

- Bring an "emergency kit" with you to the show in case you need to remove spots, trim your goat's fur or something else comes up.

- Dress appropriately for the show – you don't want to lose points for showmanship by wearing something that doesn't match the dress code of the show

Chapter Ten: Pygora Goats Care Sheet

In this chapter, you will find a few quick-reference guides for basic information regarding the care and keeping of Pygora Goats. In case you need to quickly answer a question and don't feel like flipping through the whole book, here you will find the basics on topics including:

Basic Information

Habitat/Housing Information

Feeding Guide

Breeding Information

1.) Basic Information

Scientific Name: *Capra hircus hircus*
Goat Type: Fiber
Fiber Types: mohair, cashmere, blend
Height (Does): at least 18 inches (46 cm.)
Height (Bucks): at least 23 inches (59 cm.)
Weight (Does): 65 to 75 lbs. (29 to 34 kg.)
Weight (Bucks): 75 to 95 lbs. (34 to 43 kg.)
Colors: white, black, red, cream, brown, gray
Temperament: friendly and playful
Handling: gentle and easy to handle
Lifespan: 12 to 14 years average
Other Uses: therapy animals, companion animals, pets

2.) Habitat/Housing Guide

Habitat Options: fenced-off pasture, pasture, large yard
Minimum Outdoor Space: 8.5 square meters per goat
Minimum Indoor Space: 2 square meters per goat
Fencing Materials: wood or metal posts; chain link or galvanized wire mesh fencing
Shelter Materials: wood, stone, concrete
Shelter Specifications: well-ventilated, leak-proof roof, sloped concrete floor, soft bedding

3.) Feeding Information

Type of Diet: herbivore

Main Diet: fresh hay, dry

Supplementation: other vegetables, commercial concentrates (small amount daily)

Other Needs: constant access to fresh water

Other Tips: open grazing is recommended as long as no toxic plants are accessible

4.) Breeding Information

General Information:

Sexual Maturity: 8 to 12 months

Gestation Period: 145 to 150 days

Offspring: one to four, often twins (2)

Size of Newborns: 5 lbs. (2.2 kg.)

Does

Sexual Maturity: 8 to 12 months

Ideal Breeding Age: 1 year

Breeding Weight: 60% to 75% of adult weight

Estrus: 18 to 22 days

Length of Cycle: 2 to 3 days

Signs of Heat: bleating, frequent urination, lack of appetite

Bucks

Sexual Maturity: 8 to 12 months (may become fertile as early as 8 weeks of age)

Ideal Breeding Age: 8 to 10 months

Breeding Season: July through February

Breeding Ratio: 1 buck per 25 does

Chapter Eleven: Common Mistakes Goat Owners Make

If you have never owned goats before, you should do as much research as possible to prepare yourself for the challenges involved. There is a lot that you will have to learn by experience, but there are some ways in which you can prepare yourself. In this chapter, you will find explanations of some of the most common mistakes new goat owners make so you can avoid making these same mistakes yourself.

1.) Keeping a Single Goat

All goats, not just Pygora Goats, are herd animals. This means that they must be kept in groups in order to thrive. Two goats can be kept together happily and this breed can be kept with other livestock. Wethers and does can be kept in any combination, but intact males are best kept with a wether for companionship. Pygora Goats can also be used as companion pets for cows, horses and sheep.

2.) Not Disbudding Early Enough

As was discussed earlier in the book, though certain procedures like disbudding may seem cruel, the consequences of not performing these procedures can be severe. If you fail to disbud your goats, they may end up hurting themselves during exercise or play – they may also be more likely to become entangled in ropes and nets if their horns grow in.

Disbudding your Pygora Goats is not required, but it is something you should think about – especially when the goats are young. If you wait too long to perform the procedure, it could fail. A failed disbudding is equally dangerous – if you do not perform the procedure correctly, the horns may grow in wrong and may need to be surgically removed.

3.) Inadequate Diet

The diet you offer your Pygora Goats is incredibly important. If you do not offer the right food or the right proportions of food types, your goats may fail to thrive. Goats have very sensitive stomachs and while it is often said they will eat anything, they cannot thrive on a diet of goat concentrates alone.

In order to keep your goats healthy you need to provide them with a diet containing 50% fresh hay. The remaining 50% of your goats' diet should be made up of additional vegetable matter, commercial pellets and mineral supplements. Do not make any sudden changes to your goat's diet because it could cause digestive issues.

4.) Not Castrating Male Goats

Unless you plan to breed your male goats, there is little reason not to castrate them. Castrating a male goat will prevent him from developing buck-like behavior such as aggression, head butting and urine spraying. If you do castrate your male goats, you will be able to keep them together with your does rather than housing them separately to prevent unwanted breeding.

5.) Failure to Provide Stimulus

Pygora Goats are very playful and curious by nature so they require plenty of mental stimulus. This stimulus is easy to provide by adding enrichment opportunities to the habitat. Goats love to climb, so adding some hay bales, a wagon or even some stumps to the enclosure will give them a place to play. You can also use buckets or barrels as toys for your goats to play with. Keeping your goats simulated and active is the key to keeping them happy and healthy.

Chapter Twelve: Frequently Asked Questions

In this book, you will find the answers to your questions regarding the care and keeping of Pygora Goats. In case you do not have time to flip through the whole book, or if you just want to peruse some common questions, refer to this list of frequently asked questions. These are some of the most common questions goat owners and potential goat owners ask, so read up!

Q: Do all Pygora Goats have the same type of fleece?

A: No, there are three types: A, B and C. A is mohair-like, C is cashmere-like and B is a blend of the two.

Q: What are the benefits of adopting a goat?

A: Adopting a goat rather than purchasing from a breeder can save you a lot of money. There is also the benefit that the goat is likely to have been disbudded and, in the case of male goats, castrated already. If you are lucky, the goat has also been vaccinated – all of these things will save you a lot of time and money in the long run.

Q: Do you have to shear a Pygora Goat?

A: Goats with Type A coat must be shorn because their coats do not shed (blow). You can choose whether to shear Type B and Type C coats, however, because they will shed naturally in the spring if you do not.

Q: When is the best time to shear a goat?

A: Most breeders prefer to shear in the late winter before kidding. When shearing in the winter, you must provide adequate shelter and warmth for the newly shorn goats.

Q: Can Pygora Goats be milked?

A: Yes, Pygora Goats can produce up to 1 quart (2 pints or 4 8-ounce cups) of milk per day.

Q: How often can you breed Pygora Goats?

A: Pygora Goats can be bred up to three times in 2 years. It is best, however, to give the doe a break and breed her no more than once per year.

Q: Will my goats be okay if I only feed them commercial pellets?

A: No. Fresh hay is an essential part of your goat's diet and they will not thrive without it. Ideally, fresh hay should compose 50% of your goats' diet and commercial pellets should only be used as a supplement.

Q: Do male Pygora Goats smell bad?

A: Intact males, called bucks, will develop and odor – particularly during breeding season. That odor is stronger than an Angora buck, but less harsh than a Pygmy buck.

Q: Do Pygora Goats have horns?

A: Yes, Pygora Goats have horns because both parent breeds have horns. You can, however, remove the horns if you choose to do so – but make this choice carefully and do it early for the safety of the goat.

Q: Do I have to register my goat?
A: If you want to show or breed your Pygora Goats, you must definitely register them. The parents of the goat must also be registered.

Q: Can I let my goats graze in the yard or pasture?
A: Goats are natural foragers so, if given the opportunity, they will be eager to do so. You should be careful, however, before you let your goats graze. There are certain plants which are toxic to goats so you should check your yard or pasture first to be sure it is safe.

Q: Why can't I let my goats roam free?
A: If you live on a large plot of land, you may be tempted to simply let your goats wander. There are two dangers associated with doing this. First, your goats may wander too far and become lost – they may even wander into the road and be hit by a car. Second, your goats will be

vulnerable to predators if they are not kept in a secure enclosure.

Q: To create Pygora Goats, does it matter whether the doe or buck is Pygmy or Angora?

A: No, you can breed a Pygmy buck to an Angora doe or vice versa and both matings will result in first-generation Pygora kids.

Q: When can I start breeding my goats?

A: Pygora bucks are capable of breeding as early as 4 months of age, but it is best to wait until the buck is at least 8 months and the doe at least 1 year old to breed them.

Q: What type of fencing should I use in my goat pasture?

A: There are a number of different types to choose from and many owners use a combination. Electric rope and wire helps to keep your goats in and predators out while non-climb fencing is more affordable. Field fencing and wooden rail fencing are also viable options.

Q: What are the breeding guidelines for Pygora Goats?

A: In order to be considered a true Pygora, the goat must be at least 2nd generation and must contain no more than 75% of either Pygmy or Angora ancestry.

Q: What do I need besides an enclosure for my goats?
A: In addition to the fenced enclosure itself, you will also need to provide your goats with shelter. To feed your goats, you will need a hayrack. As far as equipment goes, you may want to invest in a pair of hoof trimmers – if you plan to breed goats, you may also want to think about a disbudding iron.

Q: What should I do before buying a goat?
A: Before you go out and buy a goat, you need to be absolutely sure you can handle the commitment. Caring for goats is an everyday job – you need to provide your goats with food and fresh water, not to mention veterinary care and proper shelter. If you live in the U.K. you will need to obtain the proper permits and fill out the Animal Moving License with your chosen breeder.

Q: Can I keep Pygora Goats in a dog house?

A: You can use a large dog house as a shelter for your goats, but you cannot keep them there exclusively. These goats require plenty of space to run and play – they will not thrive if they are confined indoors for extended periods of time.

Chapter Thirteen: Relevant Websites

In case you do not find all of the information you were looking for in this book – or if you just want some extra resources – refer to the relevant websites in this chapter. Here you will find websites for feeding, care, health info, general info and showing info for Pygora Goats.

Because only goats registered with the American Angora Goat Breeders Association and the National Pygmy Goat Association are accepted as parents of Pygora Goats, this breed is fairly limited to the United States. Thus, you will find limited resources specific to the Pygora Goat under the heading "United Kingdom Websites" in the following pages. You instead finds links related to the parent breeds, Pygmy and Angora goats.

1.) Food for Pygora Goats

In this section, you will find a number of resources for feeding Pygora goats, including the types of food, how much to feed and nutritional needs.

United States Websites:

"What do Goats Eat?" Cattail Meadows.
<http://www.cattailmeadows.com/pygorafacts/pygorafacts.html#feeding>

"Capra hircus – Domestic Goat." Animal Diversity Web.
<http://animaldiversity.ummz.umich.edu/accounts/Capra_hircus/>

"Feeding Goats." Fias Co Farm.
<http://fiascofarm.com/goats/feeding.htm>

"Getting Goat Nutrition Right." Onion Creek Ranch.
<http://www.tennesseemeatgoats.com/articles2/feedinggoatsproperly.html>

United Kingdom Websites:

"Diet and Feeding." Brambles Special Breeds.
<http://www.specialbreeds.co.uk/angora-goats/caring-for-angora-goats.html>

"Goats – Feeding Your Goats." Farmgate Feeds.
<http://www.farmgatefeeds.co.uk/farmgate-product-advice-detail/goats-feeding-your-goats/aid8876447a-123a-4b83-a3ee-2b099e785b49>

"Goat Feeding Guide." Small Holder Range.
<http://www.smallholderfeed.co.uk/Healthcare-and-Management/Goat-Feeding-Guide-Original.aspx>

"Detailed Information – Goats." Fodder Solutions
<http://www.foddersolutions.co.uk/index.php?q=node/17>

2.) Care for Pygora Goats

In this section, you will find a number of resources for caring for domestic goats like the Pygora Goat, including formation about housing and fencing needs.

United States Websites:

"Pygora Care." Garrett Ranch.
<http://www.garrettranch.com/pygora_care>

"Goat Housing." CattailMeadows.
<http://www.cattailmeadows.com/pygorafacts/pygorafacts.html#housing>

"What is a Pygora Goat?" Sweet River Ranch.
<http://www.californiapygoras.com/pygoraGoat.html>

United Kingdom Websites:

"Pygora." Well Manor Farm.
<http://www.wellmanorfarm.co.uk/Southdown%20Fleece.html>

"Caring for Pygmy Goats." Goodlife Animals.
<http://www.goodlifeanimals.co.uk/page3.php>

"How to Choose and Keep Goats." CountryWide.
<http://www.countrywidefarmers.co.uk/pws/Content.ice?page=GuidesChooseKeepGoats&pgForward=businesscontentfull>

"Pygora Goat Sheering." MyDaily.
<http://www.mydaily.co.uk/video/pygora-goat-shearing>

3.) Health Info for Pygora Goats

In this section, you will find a number of resources for Pygora Goats as well as domestic goats in general, including information about common diseases, treatments and disease prevention methods.

United States Websites:

"Goat Medical Kit." Garrett Pygora.
<http://www.garrettranch.com/pygora_medical.cfm>

"Health Products." Caprine Supply.
<http://www.caprinesupply.com/products/health.html>

"Goat Health and Kidding." Hawks Mountain Ranch.
<http://www.hmrpygoras.com/goathealth.html>

"Common Diseases and Heath Problems in Sheep and Goats." Purdue University Extension.
<http://www.extension.purdue.edu/extmedia/AS/AS-595-commonDiseases.pdf>

United Kingdom Websites:

"Premium Sheep & Goat Health Schemes." Scotland's Rural College. <http://www.sruc.ac.uk/info/120113/premium_sheep_and_goat_health_schemes>

"Goat Health." Goat Veterinary Society. <http://www.goatvetsoc.co.uk/goat-health/>

"Goat Health 1 – The Healthy Goat." David Harwood BVetMEd. <http://www.nadis.org.uk/bulletins/goat-health-1-the-healthy>

"Goat Health." British Goat Society. <http://www.allgoats.org.uk/Goathealth.htm>

4.) General Info for Pygora Goats

In this section, you will find a number of resources for general information about Pygora Goats and the parent breeds.

United States Websites:

"Pygora Fiber." Pygora Breeders Association. <http://www.pygoragoats.org/Fiber.html>

"Pygora Fleece Types." Hawks Mountain Ranch Pygora Goats. <http://www.hmrpygoras.com/HMRPygoraFleeceTypesweb.html>

"Pygora University." Garrett Ranch. <http://www.garrettranch.com/pygora_university.cfm>

"About Pygora Fiber." Amity Creek Pygora. <http://amitycreekpygora.com/about_fiber>

"Pygora Goat." Oregon Zoo. <http://www.oregonzoo.org/discover/animals/pygora-goat>

United Kingdom Websites:

"Angora Goats." Rare Breeds Goats.
<http://www.rarebreedgoats.co.uk/angora-goats>

"The Pygmy Goat." Renn.co.uk.
<http://www.renn.co.uk/pg4.html>

"History of Angora Goats." British Angora Goat Society.
<http://www.angoragoats-mohair>

"Capra hircus – Pygmy Goat." Woburn Safari Park.
<http://www.woburnsafari.co.uk/discover/meet-the-animals/mammals/pygmy-goat/>

5.) *Showing Pygora Goats*

In this section, you will find a number of resources for showing goats, including breed standard information, showing tips and guides for moving goats to show grounds.

United States Websites:

"Shows/Events." Pygora Breeders Association.
<http://www.pygoragoats.org/Shows.html>

"Showing Products." Caprine Supply.
<http://www.caprinesupply.com/products/showing>

"Breed Standard." Pygora Breeders Association.
<http://www.pygoragoats.org/BreedStandard.html>

United Kingdom Websites:

"Showing Goats." Small Holder Range.
<http://www.smallholderfeed.co.uk/articles/showing>

"A Beginner's Guide to Showing Goats." Scottish Smallholder & Grower Festival.

<http://www.scottishsmallholdershow.co.uk/beginners-guide-to-showing>

"Goat Showing." Goats.co.uk.
<http://www.goats.co.uk/Goat_Showing.htm>

"Guidance for Keepers in England and Wales: Sheep and Goats: Movements to Show Grounds." Gov.uk.
<https://www.gov.uk/government/publications/guidance-for-keepers-in-england-and-wales-sheep-and-goats-movements-to-show-grounds>

Index

Q

R

S

T

U

V

W

Y

Photo Credits

Title Page PhotoBy Flickr user Jdsmith1021, <http://www.flickr.com/photos/jdsmith1021/7892405032/sizes/m/in/photostream/>

Page 1 Photo By April from usa (goat) [CC-BY-2.0 (http://creativecommons.org/licenses/by/2.0)], via Wikimedia Commons, <http://commons.wikimedia.org/wiki/File:Pygora_goat_Oregon_Zoo.jpg>

Page 5 Photo By Marianne Madden via Wikimedia Commons, <http://en.m.wikipedia.org/wiki/File:Oregon_Zoo_White_Goat.jpg>

Page 13 Photo By Ltshears - Trisha M Shears (Own work) [Public domain], via Wikimedia Commons, <http://commons.wikimedia.org/wiki/File:African_Pygmy_Goat_003.jpg>

Page 14 Photo by Erica Peterson via Wikimedia Commons, <http://en.wikipedia.org/wiki/File:Quebec_angora_goat.jpg

Page 15 Photo By Paul Esson (http://www.flickr.com/photos/paulesson/2353307653/)

Page 41 Photo By Flickr user ArranET,
<http://www.flickr.com/photos/arran_edmonstone_photography/4995279544/sizes/m/in/photostream/>

Page 50 Photo By Flickr user Havankevin,
<http://www.flickr.com/photos/marionenkevin/508284886/sizes/m/in/photostream/>

Page 55 Photo By Flickr user Moonrat42,
<http://www.flickr.com/photos/moonrat/2450166522/sizes/m/in/photostream/>

Page 59 Photo By Mistvan (Own work) [GFDL (http://www.gnu.org/copyleft/fdl.html) or CC-BY-SA-3.0-2.5-2.0-1.0 (http://creativecommons.org/licenses/by-sa/3.0)], via Wikimedia Commons,
<http://commons.wikimedia.org/wiki/File:Young.Pygmy>

Page 60 Photo Via Wikimedia Commons,
<http://en.wikipedia.org/wiki/File:Suckling_goat.jpg>

Page 66 Photo By Ken Hammond via Wikimedia Commons,
<http://en.wikipedia.org/wiki/File:Wool.www.usda.gov.jpg

Page 68 Photo By David Wilmot from Wimbledon, United Kingdom (Flickr) [CC-BY-2.0

(http://creativecommons.org/licenses/by/2.0)], via Wikimedia Commons, <http://commons.wikimedia.org/wiki/File:Wool_Spinning.jpg>

Page 71 Photo By Flickr user RoundedbyGravity, <http://www.flickr.com/photos/unfoldedorigami/3096126107/sizes/m/in/photostream/>

Page 78 Photo By Flickr user WingedBlue, <http://www.flickr.com/photos/wingedblue/5574354061/sizes/m/in/photostream/>

Page 92 Photo By Flickr user Bella Remy Photography, <http://www.flickr.com/photos/bellaremyphotography/9594822054/sizes/m/in/photostream/>

Page 100 Photo By Flickr user WingedBlue, <http://www.flickr.com/photos/wingedblue/5574351451/sizes/m/in/photostream/>

Page 104 Photo By Flickr user Leunix, <http://www.flickr.com/photos/leunix/228389019/sizes/m/in/photostream/>

Page 108 Photo By Flickr user Tambako the Jaguar, <http://www.flickr.com/photos/tambako/4384817853/sizes/m/in/photostream/>

Page 115 Photo By Ltshears – Trisha M Shears, via Wikimedia Commons, <http://en.wikipedia.org/wiki/File:Angora>

References

"A Beginner's Guide to Showing Goats." Scottish Smallholder & Grower Festival. <http://www.scottishsmallholdershow.co.uk/beginners-guide-to-showing>

"A Goat of a Different Color and Fleece Too!" Hawks Mountain Ranch. <http://www.hmrpygoras.com/HMRPygoraFleeceTypesweb.html>

"Breed Standards." Garret Ranch. <http://www.garrettranch.com/breed>

"Breeds of Livestock." Oklahoma State University, Department of Animal Science. <http://www.ansi.okstate.edu/breeds/goats/>

"Common Diseases and Heath Problems in Sheep and Goats." Purdue University Extension. <http://www.extension.purdue.edu/extmedia/AS/AS-595-commonDiseases.pdf>

"Goat Glossary of Terms." Goat-Link. <http://goat-link.com/content/view/24/#.UqewLfRDszA>

"Goat Medical Kit." Garrett Pygora. <http://www.garrettranch.com/pygora_medical.cfm>

"Harvesting Pygora." Pygora Goat Breeders Association. <http://www.pygoragoats.org/Fiber_Havesting.html>

Harwood, David. "The Healthy Goat." BVetMEd. <http://www.nadis.org.uk/bulletins/goat-health-1-the-healthy>

"How the Spinning Wheel Works." The Joy of Handspinning. <http://joyofhandspinning.com/how-the-spinning>

"Keeping Goats in Small Spaces." My Urban Homestead. <https://wooddogs3.wordpress.com/tag/keeping-goats-in-small-spaces/>

Mitchell, Elise R. "Brush Control with Goats." The Kerr Center. <http://www.kerrcenter.com/publications/brushcontrol_goats.html>

"Mohair." AngoraGoat.com. <http://angoragoat.com/mohair>

Pfalzbot, Gary. "Brush Control Using Goats." Goat World.
<http://www.goatworld.com/articles/brushcontrol/brushcontrol.shtml>

"Prenatal Care – Preparation for Kidding & Signs of Labor."
Fias Co Farm.
<http://fiascofarm.com/goats/prenatalcare.html>

"Pygora Goat." Oregon Zoo.
<http://www.oregonzoo.org/discover/animals/pygora-goat>

"Questions and Answers About Pygora Goats." Hawks
Mountain Ranch Pygora Goats.
<http://www.hmrpygoras.com/PBAquestionsAnswers398.html>

"Sheep and Goats." Animal Health and Veterinary
Laboratories Agency. <http://www.defra.gov.uk/ahvla-en/keeping-animals/registering/sheep-goats/>

"The Story of PBA – A Story of Fluff." Pygora Breeders
Association.
<http://www.pygoragoats.org/PBA_Story.html>

"What is a Pygora Goat?" Sweet River Ranch.
<http://www.californiapygoras.com/pygoraGoat.html>

www.ingramcontent.com/pod-product-compliance
Lightning Source LLC
LaVergne TN
LVHW021341080426
835508LV00020B/2065